**Quick Start Guides**

C000273403

The Essential
SUGAR FREE DIET
COOKBOOK

A Quick Start Guide To Sugar Free Cooking

Over 100 New and Delicious Sugar-Free Recipes!

First published in 2015 by Erin Rose Publishing

Text and illustration copyright © 2015 Erin Rose Publishing

Design: Julie Anson

ISBN: 978-0-9928232-7-6

A CIP record for this book is available from the British Library.

DISCLAIMER: This book is for informational purposes only and not intended as a substitute for the medical advice, diagnosis or treatment of a physician or qualified healthcare provider. The reader should consult a physician before undertaking a new health care regimen and in all matters relating to his/her health, and particularly with respect to any symptoms that may require diagnosis or medical attention.

While every care has been taken in compiling the recipes for this book we cannot accept responsibility for any problems which arise as a result of preparing one of the recipes. The author and publisher disclaim responsibility for any adverse effects that may arise from the use or application of the recipes in this book. Some of the recipes in this book include nuts and eggs. If you have an egg or nut allergy it's important to avoid these. It is recommended that children, pregnant women, the elderly or anyone who has an immune system disorder avoid eating raw eggs.

CONTENTS

Recipes

Dinner

Snacks, Desserts & Sweet Treats

Sauces & Dips

INTRODUCTION

As a result of the huge success of **'What Can I Eat On A Sugar Free Diet?'**, we now bring you **'The Essential Sugar Free Diet Cookbook'**, with another 100 healthy, delicious and sugar-free recipes!

If you already have the first book, then these 100 new recipes will help you maintain your sugar-free lifestyle with tons of new and delicious sugar-free recipe ideas, plus a reminder of the sugar contents of fruit, so that you have all the information in one place.

For those of you who are starting out on a sugar-free diet - welcome! You've made a great choice, and we're here to help you get started! A sugar-free diet doesn't have to lack flavour and excitement, or even take a long time to prepare. Here you will find plenty of satisfying meal ideas; from warm, nourishing root vegetable soups and sweet tasting curries and casseroles, right though to healthy snacks and delicious deserts – all enough to satisfy you without the use of harmful ingredients or added sugar.

Our recipes are quick, easy and delicious! Simple is the way forward.
Up for the challenge? Let's do it.

What Can I Eat On A Sugar Free Diet?

Don't Eat These:

Any food containing sugar.

- Avoid all fizzy and sugary drinks, including diet drinks with artificial sweeteners such as, aspartame, xylitol, sucralose, cyclamates, saccharin, acesulfame potassium

- Avoid dried fruit, including apricots, dates, raisins, sultanas, apples, bananas, mangoes, pineapples, figs etc.

- Pure or concentrated fruit juices

- Cakes, biscuits, muesli, granola, muffins, cereal bars and sweets

- Breakfast cereals (where sugar is added to the ingredients)

- Sucrose

- Maltose

- Dextrose

- Corn syrup

- Glucose syrup

- Fructose

- High fructose corn syrup

- Agave syrup or nectar

- Honey

- Jam

- Golden syrup

- Maple syrup

- Treacle

- Molasses

- Ready-made sauces like relish, ketchup and barbecue sauce

Do Eat These:

Eat some protein with every meal. It staves off hunger and has less of an effect on blood sugar. Keep fruit to a maximum of 2 pieces a day and opt for the lower sugar fruits. It may be easier to avoid fruit completely to begin with.

- Chicken, pork, lamb, turkey and beef
- Prawns, cod, salmon, and mackerel – oily fish are especially good.
- Uncoated nuts; Brazils, hazelnuts, cashews, peanuts and pecans
- Sunflower, sesame and pumpkin seeds
- Cheese
- Yogurt
- Eggs
- Nut butters; peanut, almond and cashew
- All fresh vegetables (Note; beetroot, carrots and onions are higher in sugar so reduce or avoid too much of these if you're struggling with cravings and watching your weight)
- Raspberries, blueberries, kiwi, blackberries, rhubarb, lime and lemons
- Brown rice, quinoa and wholemeal bread (check label for added sugar)
- Popcorn
- Herbal and fruit teas (check for added sugar)
- Remove sugar from tea and coffee
- Corn
- Coconut oil
- Coconut flakes
- Olive oil
- Tinned tuna and sardines
- Cooked chicken, prawns or ham which you can nibble on

How To Read The Labels

So you pick up cooked chicken in the supermarket, thinking it's just chicken, right? Wrong. Often during cooking, chicken and other meats have been basted with a sugary sauce or glaze. Cooked meats like Chinese or barbeque chicken have almost certainly been coated in a marinade containing sugar.

Sugar can also be listed under the names below. Avoid these.

- Invert sugar syrup
- Cane juice crystals
- Dextrin
- Dextrose
- Glucose syrup
- Sucrose
- Fructose syrup
- Maltodextrin
- Barley malt
- Beet sugar
- High fructose corn syrup
- Corn syrup
- Date sugar
- Palm sugar or coconut sugar
- Malt syrup
- Dehydrated fruit juice
- Fruit juice concentrate
- Carob syrup
- Golden syrup
- Refiners syrup
- Ethyl maltol
- Jaggery

The Fructose Facts

If you are already well informed and experienced in how to cut out sugar, it won't come as a surprise to you that fructose, a type of sugar which is found in fruit, can only be broken down and stored in the liver and is actually bad for you.

However, we do need to differentiate between naturally occurring fructose and the types of sugar products which have undergone a factory process, stripped of nutrients, concentrated and altered which then becomes harmful to the body. The first well known culprit which comes to mind is high fructose corn syrup which is commonly linked with various health problems. Many of us link the word 'fructose' with natural fruit sugar and mentally tick it off as being OK to eat. This is not the case.

OTHER SWEETENERS

Other types of sweeteners, natural and unnatural, also have implications, and for many people it requires a decisive choice as to what sweetener they wish to use. For some, honey is a clear winner because it's natural, could have health benefits and can be added to a variety of meals. But the flip side is that it does contain fructose and glucose; but for many people it's the lesser of various evils. Others tend to opt for the artificial sweeteners because they are calorie free and easy to use. We've been led to believe that agave syrup, which many of us have been using as a low GI sugar substitute, was a healthy suitable alternative to sugar making agave a vote-winner for years. However, now research has shown it's actually on a par with high fructose corn syrup, due to its processing and high concentration of fructose.

The main difference between fructose and glucose is that the body utilises glucose immediately whereas fructose is stored in the liver and becomes fat. Despite containing fructose, the benefits of whole, fresh fruit can't be neglected. Furthermore, when fruit is consumed with its natural fibre it reduces the effect on the body. The fibre causes the fruit sugar to be absorbed more slowly, therefore it won't cause sugar spikes in the same way as a glass of concentrated orange juice. And let's be smart about this, fruit is packed with goodness and the fibre is an aid to healthy digestion. Unlike refined sugar products it doesn't contain empty calories. Fruit really plays an essential role in a balanced diet.

In our recipes we don't use potentially harmful artificial sweeteners and there is no added sugar; we really believe that a healthy diet is based on clean eating, avoiding processed foods and keeping sugar consumption to a minimum.

We do give you the option to use stevia, a sweetener extracted from the Stevia Rebaudiana plant which has no known harmful effects, but for those of you who don't like the taste we have plenty of other options. Adding sweetness naturally to a recipe is our goal!

the Sugar Content Of Fruit

Some of the recipes included in this book do have fruit in them and it's sometimes best to hold back on these recipes until you feel confident that you're in control of your sugar consumption. Just be aware that eating something sweet, regardless of it being natural or artificial, can trigger cravings for other sweet things.

Some people benefit from avoiding fruit entirely for the first 2-4 weeks while their taste buds adjust. After that, you may want to experiment and treat yourself to something sweet. We've included a list of the sugar content of fruit, so you can choose how strict you wish to be. If you are insulin resistant or trying to lose weight you may wish to avoid some of these. But let's be sensible about this and not worry too much about the numbers. Having a couple of pieces of whole fruit is nowhere near as harmful as adding refined sugars and fibre-free fructose. Some of you will prefer to let go a little on the fruit because giving up refined sugars was your intention and if that works for you, great. The nutrients from fruit are valuable and the taste sensation is important to add variety to your diet, not to mention pure enjoyment.

Dried fruit has a higher sugar content than fresh, and the best way to eat fruit is in its whole, natural state as the fibre will slow down its absorption. Pure fruit juices and those from concentrate, are basically liquid fructose and will result in higher blood sugar, upsetting your blood sugar balance. It's the swing that can create unexplained mood swings, shakiness and fatigue.

Sugar Content Of Fruit Per 100g

Figs 16g

Grapes 16g

Lychee 15g

Mango 14g

Pomegranate 14g

Banana...12g

Pineapple 10g

Apple 10g

Blueberries 10g

Kiwi fruit 9g

Orange 9g

Cherries 8g

Papaya 8g

Peach 8g

Nectarine 8g

Honeydew melon 8g

Watermelon...6g

Strawberries 4.9g

Blackberries 4.9g

Raspberries 4.4g

Lemon 2.5g

Lime 1.7g

Rhubarb 1.1g

4g of sugar = 1 teaspoon

The guide will allow you to select which fruits to choose when you reintroduce fruit into your diet. Fruit has great nutritional value, but 100g of raspberries only has a quarter of the sugar of figs, so choose wisely and you can still keep your sugar intake low and have fresh fruit every day. The sugar content of vegetables is generally much lower than in fruit. Sweet tasting vegetables often thought to be high in sugar are still lower than that of many fruits. Carrots come in at 4.7g, pumpkin at 2.8g and spinach at 0.4g. However beetroot, even unsweetened, has a sugar content of 7g, almost as much as honeydew melon.

Can I Drink Alcohol?

With many alcoholic drinks, it's the mixers which are high in sugar and are difficult, if not impossible, to avoid if you drink spirits. Soda water is about your only option as a mixer, with a squeeze of fresh lemon or lime added. Cider, liqueurs and dessert wine can be very high in sugar. Vodka, gin and dry wine have less sugar. In the early days of going sugar-free it's may be wise to avoid alcohol altogether. Plus, if you over-do it, a resulting hangover could set you back with a bout of sugar cravings.

Get Ready For Sugar-Freedom!

What Should I Expect When I Cut Out Sugar?

So, let's not sugar coat this! Expect some cravings to start with. If you've been eating what is classed today as a normal diet, you've probably been consuming too much sugar, and that's without adding it to your breakfast cereal or coffee; it's hard to avoid it.

Cravings vary in degree, depending on your current sugar consumption. Your taste buds need to adjust to experiencing natural flavours rather than powerfully sweet empty calories. So while you are adjusting, distract yourself, think of something else, get some exercise, snack on protein rich foods like nuts, cheese, cold meats and drink plenty of water. Taking a walk will keep you away from the kitchen.

Tips For Going Sugar-Free

If sugar cravings kick in well before your next meal, apart from snacking on something high protein one of the best ways to overcome cravings is to use distraction. Literally, get up and do something.

- Getting some exercise really helps! Don't sit around waiting for the onset of sugar cravings. Even gentle exercise like walking, swimming or cycling.

- Snack on protein instead of carbohydrates. Carry on-the-go snacks like nuts, olives, cheese, or cooked meat for quick sustenance.

- At mealtimes, replace starchy carbohydrates with lots of veggies and you'll not only feel less sluggish but less hungry too.

- Eating little and often is great. Five meals/snacks a day is best but watch your portion sizes.

- Drink plenty of water!

- Prepare some cucumber water. Steep sliced cucumber and mint leaves in a large jug of water, store in the fridge and serve with ice and lemon.

- Prepare meals and treats for the fridge or freezer. Have something sugar-free close by so that you aren't tempted.

- Get plenty of rest and sleep.

- Start your day with a protein breakfast like eggs and bacon.

- Watch your starchy food and carbohydrate consumption, especially flour products.

- High protein foods can help break the cravings for not only sugar but starchy carbohydrates like white bread, biscuits and cakes.

Recipes

Sugar-Free Cooking

With so many recipes to choose from we hope you find something to entice you which you can add to your list of favourites. Many of our recipes are not only sugar-free but also gluten-free as we know many of you like to avoid wheat and gluten too. Where dairy milk is added you can swap it for non-dairy alternatives like almond, soya or rice milk.

For your store cupboard basics you could stock up on a range of herbs and spices because when you're reducing one flavour in your food you might want to replace it with another. Fresh herbs have a better flavour but if you can't access them, dried ones will suffice.

Cinnamon and vanilla are great store-cupboard essentials with a long shelf life. Vanilla pods can be expensive but vanilla extracts can contain sugar so make sure you read the labels. Having coconut oil and coconut milk in your cupboard plus keeping a stock of nuts, seeds and herbs can really open up your cooking options and add delicious flavours to your dishes.

In some of our recipes we've used whole fruit as a sweetener, together with its fibre, so you get the nutrition and the bonus of the sweetness, which when combined with the other ingredients, won't elevate your blood sugar excessively.

Experiment until your meals are right for you. Enjoy!

BREAKFAST

Quinoa & Blueberry Porridge

Ingredients

- 50g (2oz) quinoa, cooked
- 50g (2oz) rolled oats
- 50g (2oz) blueberries
- 250ml (8floz) almond or soya milk
- 2 tablespoons pumpkin seeds
- 2 tablespoons flaked almonds

SERVES 1

Method

Place the oats, quinoa and milk in a saucepan. Bring to the boil and cook for 5 minutes until it thickens. Serve topped off with blueberries, pumpkin seeds and almonds.

Chilled Raspberry Porridge

Ingredients

- 50g (2oz) raspberries
- 50g (2oz) rolled oats
- 200ml (7floz) coconut milk
- 40g (1 ½ oz) chia seeds
- 100ml (3 ½ floz) water

SERVES 1

Method

Place the raspberries, oats, coconut milk and water into a blender and process until smooth. Stir in the chia seeds and mix well. Chill before serving. Serve with coconut shavings and raspberries. This is a great breakfast for summer mornings which can be prepared the night before.

Spanish Tortilla

Ingredients

2 tablespoons olive oil

1 onion, finely chopped

200g (7oz) new potatoes, cooked and roughly chopped

6 eggs

2 tablespoons fresh parsley, chopped

2 tablespoons fresh basil, chopped

Freshly ground black pepper

SERVES 4

Method

Heat the oil in a frying pan. Add the onion and cook until soft. Add the potatoes and warm through. In a separate bowl, whisk the eggs then add the parsley, basil and pepper. Pour the egg mixture into the pan on top of the onions and potatoes. Stir briefly then allow the eggs to set for around 3 minutes or until the mixture is firm. When you are sure it is cooked through, place a plate on top of the pan and tip out the tortilla. Serve with salad. It can be served warm or cold and makes a great lunch box option.

Almond & Nectarine Yogurt

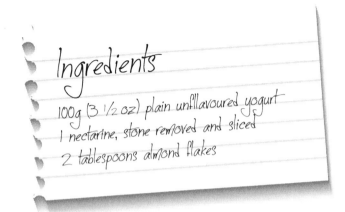

SERVES 1

Ingredients

100g (3 ½ oz) plain unfllavoured yogurt
1 nectarine, stone removed and sliced
2 tablespoons almond flakes

Method

Put half of the nectarine slices into a glass; add a layer of yogurt topped with a sprinkling of almond flakes, followed by another layer of the same. Eat straight away.

Blackberry Crunch

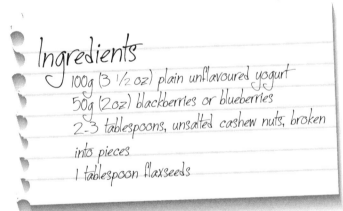

SERVES 1

Ingredients

100g (3 ½ oz) plain unflavoured yogurt
50g (2oz) blackberries or blueberries
2-3 tablespoons, unsalted cashew nuts, broken
into pieces
1 tablespoon flaxseeds

Method

Mash together half of the blackberries with the yogurt and flaxseeds. Using a glass, place a layer of yogurt with some of the whole blackberries you held back and a sprinkling of cashews, followed by another layer of the same until you reach the top of the glass. Garnish with cashew pieces and a blackberry or two.

Courgette (Zucchini) Scramble

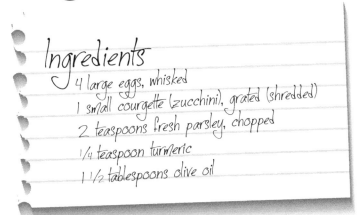

Ingredients

4 large eggs, whisked
1 small courgette (zucchini), grated (shredded)
2 teaspoons fresh parsley, chopped
1/4 teaspoon turmeric
1 1/2 tablespoons olive oil

SERVES
2

Method

Heat the oil in a frying pan, sprinkle in the turmeric and stir. Add the courgette (zucchini) to the pan and cook for 2 minutes. Pour in the eggs and stir the mixture until it's lightly scrambled. Sprinkle with parsley and serve.

Apple & Cheese Omelette

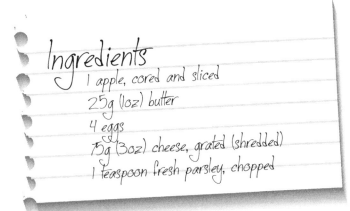

Ingredients

1 apple, cored and sliced
25g (1oz) butter
4 eggs
75g (3oz) cheese, grated (shredded)
1 teaspoon fresh parsley, chopped

SERVES
2

Method

Heat the butter in a frying pan, add the apple and cook until soft then set aside. Whisk the eggs and sprinkle in the parsley. Pour the beaten eggs into the pan and cook until they are soft but set. Add the apple slices and cheese to the omelette, fold it over to allow the cheese to melt before serving..

Raspberry Pancakes

Ingredients

- 175g (6oz) self-raising flour
- 2 eggs, beaten
- 250ml (8fl oz) milk
- 200g (7oz) raspberries
- Juice of 1 lemon
- 1 tablespoon coconut oil or olive oil

SERVES
2

Method

Mix together the eggs, milk and raspberries in a bowl. Place the flour in a bowl, make a well in the centre and pour in the egg mixture. Whisk until you have a smooth batter. If you have time, leave to stand for 20 minutes. Heat some olive oil in a pan, pour in some batter mix and cook until the pancake bubbles and becomes golden underneath. Turn it over and cook for around a minute. Repeat for the remaining pancake mixture. Serve warm with a squeeze of lemon juice.

Beetroot & Apple Smoothie

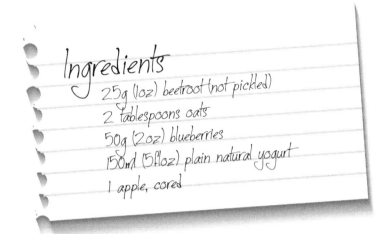

Ingredients
- 25g (1oz) beetroot (not pickled)
- 2 tablespoons oats
- 50g (2oz) blueberries
- 150ml (5floz) plain natural yogurt
- 1 apple, cored

SERVES
1

Method

Place all the ingredients into a blender and blitz until smooth. Serve in a tall glass.

Raspberry & Coconut Smoothie

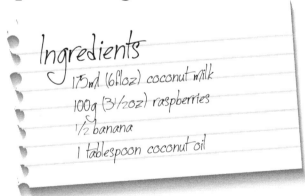

Ingredients
- 175ml (6floz) coconut milk
- 100g (3½oz) raspberries
- ½ banana
- 1 tablespoon coconut oil

SERVES
1

Method

Toss all of the ingredients into a blender. Blitz until creamy. Pour and enjoy!

Carrot & Ginger Smoothie

Ingredients
- 1 carrot
- 1 apple
- 2.5cm (1 inch) chunk of fresh ginger root

SERVES
1

Method

Place all the ingredients into a smoothie maker or blender and add enough water to cover them. Blitz until smooth.

Avocado & Orange Smoothie

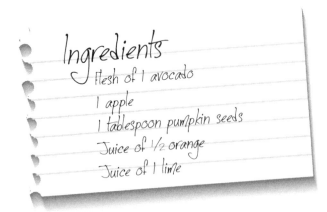

Ingredients
- flesh of 1 avocado
- 1 apple
- 1 tablespoon pumpkin seeds
- Juice of 1/2 orange
- Juice of 1 lime

SERVES
1

Method

Put all the ingredients into a blender with just enough water to cover the ingredients. Blitz until smooth.

Creamy Kale Smoothie

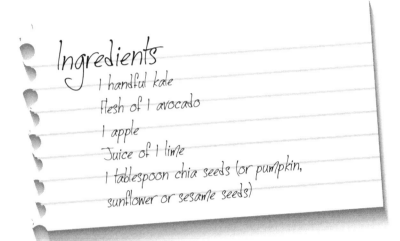

Ingredients
- 1 handful kale
- flesh of 1 avocado
- 1 apple
- Juice of 1 lime
- 1 tablespoon chia seeds (or pumpkin, sunflower or sesame seeds)

SERVES
1

Method

Place all the ingredients into a food processor with enough water to cover and blitz until smooth.

Pear Porridge

Ingredients
- 50g (2oz) porridge oats
- 250ml (8fl oz) milk or dairy free alternative
- 1/4 teaspoon ground cinnamon
- 1/2 pear, peeled and chopped
- 1 tablespoon hazelnuts, chopped

SERVES
1

Method

Apart from the nuts, place all the other ingredients, in a saucepan and cook for 5 minutes or until it thickens. Serve the porridge and sprinkle with hazelnuts.

Spinach & Poached Eggs

Ingredients
- 2 large eggs
- 1 large handful of fresh spinach
- Sea salt and pepper to taste

SERVES 1

Method

Bring a pan of water to boil, add the spinach and cook for 1 minute. Drain the spinach and keep warm. Bring a shallow pan of water to the boil, add an egg and poach for about 5 minutes, or until whites are firm. Serve the eggs on top of the spinach and season with salt and pepper.

Cauliflower Hash

Ingredients
- 1 cauliflower, washed and grated (shredded)
- 1 small onion, finely chopped
- 1 teaspoon butter
- 1/2 teaspoon paprika
- Sea salt and pepper

SERVES 4

Method

Heat the butter in a frying pan and add the onion. Cook until the onion becomes soft. Add the grated cauliflower. Stir and cook until the cauliflower is tender and golden brown. Add some extra butter if you need to. Season with paprika, salt and pepper and serve.

Sweet Breakfast Risotto

Ingredients

200g (7oz) risotto rice (Arborio)
400ml (14fl oz) water
1 x 400ml (14fl oz) tin of coconut milk
225g (8oz) pineapple, diced
50g (2oz) flaked (sliced) almonds
1 banana, sliced

SERVES
4

Method

Bring the water and rice to the boil, reduce the heat and simmer. While the rice is cooking prepare the rest of the ingredients. Once the rice has softened, add in the pineapple and coconut milk. Cook until creamy then add in the banana. Heat it through and the breakfast risotto is ready to serve when it's soft and creamy. This can be served hot or cold and the fruit or nuts you use can be varied.

Breakfast Bake

Ingredients

2 tablespoons olive oil
8 top quality sausages
1 sweet potato, peeled and diced
1 onion, chopped
2 handfuls of spinach
10 eggs, beaten
1/2 teaspoon paprika
1/2 teaspoon garlic powder

SERVES
6

Method

Heat the olive oil in a frying pan and add the diced sweet potato. Stir and cook until soft. Transfer the sweet potato to a casserole dish. Place the sausages and onion into the pan and fry until the sausages are cooked through. Transfer them to the casserole dish. Add in the spinach leaves, eggs, paprika and garlic powder and mix well. Bake in the oven at 200C/400F for around 30 minutes until the eggs are completely set.

LUNCH

Pear, Walnuts & Blue Cheese Salad

SERVES 2

Ingredients

2 pears, peeled
1 teaspoon olive oil
1 teaspoon butter
½ teaspoon ground coriander
125g (4oz) green salad leaves
25g (1oz) blue cheese, crumbled
2 tablespoon walnuts, roughly chopped
1 tablespoon lemon juice

Method

Wash the pears and cut in half. Remove the core then cut each half into quarters. Heat the oil and butter in a pan. Add the pears and walnuts. Cook for 3 minutes until the pears are soft. Sprinkle with the ground coriander. Toss in a bowl with the salad leaves and lemon juice. Sprinkle in the blue cheese. Serve immediately and enjoy.

Bacon Wrapped Asparagus

Ingredients

14 asparagus spears
7 slices of Parma ham, cut in half
Oil for greasing the baking sheet

SERVES
2

Method

Wrap each asparagus stalk with a slice of Parma ham. Coat a baking sheet with oil and lay the asparagus wraps on the sheet. Bake at 200C /400F for 10-12 minutes, until the asparagus has softened and the ham is crispy. Alternatively, put a thin slice of cheese between the asparagus and ham before cooking.

Tuna & Haricot Bean Salad

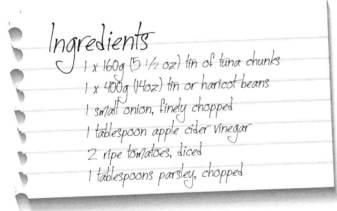

Ingredients

1 x 160g (5 1/2 oz) tin of tuna chunks
1 x 400g (14oz) tin or haricot beans
1 small onion, finely chopped
1 tablespoon apple cider vinegar
2 ripe tomatoes, diced
1 tablespoons parsley, chopped

SERVES
2

Method

Combine all of the ingredients in a bowl. Season with salt and pepper and serve.

Chicory & Fennel Salad

Ingredients

1 large fennel bulb, finely chopped
1 chicory bulb, sliced
1 small lambs lettuce, chopped
2 spring onions (scallions) chopped
Zest of 1 large orange and the flesh
chopped
1 tablespoons red wine vinegar
2 tablespoons olive oil

SERVES
2

Method

Place the lettuce, chicory and spring onions (scallions) into a bowl. In a separate bowl mix together the olive oil, vinegar and orange zest. Mix the dressing well and season with salt and pepper. Place the fennel and orange flesh into the dressing and mix well. Pour the dressing, fennel and orange over the salad and toss it. Chill before serving.

Prawn Soufflé Omelette

Ingredients

75g (3oz) cooked, peeled prawns
1 courgette (zucchini) grated (shredded)
4 eggs, whites separated from yolks
1 tablespoon fresh chives
1-2 tablespoons olive oil

SERVES
2

Method

Blot the excess moisture off the courgette (zucchini) using kitchen paper. Beat the egg whites until they form stiff peaks and set aside. Beat the egg yolks separately. Fold the egg yolks into the whisked egg whites. Heat the olive oil in a frying pan. Add the prawns and courgettes (zucchinis) and fry for 2 minutes. Pour in the eggs and cook until they have set. Serve topped with a sprinkling of chives.

Tuna, Avocado & Lettuce Wraps

SERVES 2

Ingredients

6 firm lettuce leaves, preferably Romaine
or Iceberg lettuce
1 x 160g (5 ½ oz) tin of tuna
1 avocado, peeled and cubed
½ cucumber, thinly sliced
¼ teaspoon paprika
Squeeze of lemon juice
Sea salt and freshly ground black pepper

Method

Combine the tuna, avocado, paprika and lemon juice in a bowl. Season with salt and pepper. Take a lettuce leaf and line it with cucumber slices and top it off with a scoop of the tuna mixture. Eat straight away. The combinations you can use for lettuce wraps are endless. You could try bacon, cheese and tomato or use leftover chicken, chilli or beef and add a dollop of guacamole for a deliciously light but filling lunch.

Kale, Swede & Crispy Bacon

Ingredients

175g (6oz) bacon,
700g (1lb 9 oz) swede, diced
500g (1lb 2oz) kale
1 clove of garlic, crushed
25g (1oz) butter
Sea salt
Freshly ground black pepper

SERVES 4

Method

Cover the swede with boiling water and cook until tender. In the meantime, remove any tough stalks from the kale and chop the leaves finely. Cover the kale with boiling water and cook for around 4-5 minutes until it softens. Drain off the water then set aside. Meanwhile, grill (broil) the bacon until crispy. Melt the butter in a frying pan, add the garlic and cook for 1 minute. Stir in the cooked kale and swede. Chop the crispy bacon and scatter through the vegetables. Toss everything together in the pan and season with salt and pepper before serving. It can also be served with a sprinkling of cheese on top.

Prawn & Avocado Salad

Ingredients

1lb (450g) cooked medium sized prawns (shrimp)

1 tomato, de-seeded and chopped

3 spring onions (scallions) chopped

1 clove of garlic, crushed

2 tablespoons lemon juice

1 large ripe avocado or 2 small ones, diced

1 tablespoon fresh mint, chopped

2 tablespoons pumpkin seeds, chopped

Pinch cayenne pepper

1 head small Romaine lettuce, outer leaves removed

SERVES 4

Method

If the prawns (shrimps) have been frozen make sure they are completely defrosted. Pat them dry with paper towels. In a large bowl, mix together all of the ingredients. Chill for at least 20 minutes before serving onto a bed of chopped lettuce.

Lentil Soup

Ingredients

- 175g (6oz) red lentils
- 1 litre (1 ½ pints) water
- 1 bay leaf
- 2 tablespoons olive oil
- 1 clove of garlic, crushed
- 1 onion, chopped
- 2 carrots, chopped
- 2 sticks of celery, chopped
- 1 teaspoon ground coriander
- ½ teaspoon turmeric
- ½ teaspoon ground cumin
- ½ teaspoon chilli powder

**SERVES
6**

Method

Heat the olive oil in a saucepan and add the cumin and onion. Cook for 5 minutes to soften the onion. Add the garlic, celery and carrots and cook for 10 minutes. Add all the remaining spices and the bay leaf and cook for 2 minutes. Add the lentils then pour in the water. Bring to the boil, reduce the heat and simmer for 50 minutes. Remove the bay leaf then transfer the soup to a blender and process until smooth. Return the soup to the saucepan and heat it thoroughly. Season and serve.

Chicken Noodle Soup

Ingredients

150g (5oz) cooked chicken, shredded (leftovers are fine)

125g (4oz) rice noodles,

100ml (3½ floz) coconut milk

1 tablespoon curry paste

2 onions, finely chopped

2 cloves of garlic, chopped

2 litres (3 pints) chicken stock (broth)

3 tablespoons fresh coriander (cilantro), chopped

Zest of 1 lime

1 tablespoon olive oil

SERVES 4-6

Method

Heat the oil in a saucepan and stir in the curry paste. Add the garlic, onions and lime with a tablespoon of stock (broth). Cook for around 5 minutes until the onion has softened. Add to the saucepan the chicken and the remaining stock. Bring to the boil then add the rice noodles. Reduce the heat and simmer for around 3 minutes or until the noodles are cooked. Stir in the coriander (cilantro) and coconut milk and warm it through. Season and serve.

Smoked Haddock Chowder

Ingredients

1 onion, finely chopped

350g (12oz) smoked haddock,

250g (9 oz) shelled raw prawns (shrimps)

200g (7oz) smoked bacon, finely chopped

2 large potatoes, peeled and diced

2 tablespoons cornflour

250ml (8floz) double cream (heavy cream)

600ml (1 pint) vegetable or fish stock (broth)

300g (11oz) sweetcorn

25g (1oz) butter

1 bay leaf

SERVES 4

Method

Heat the butter in a frying pan and add the onion. Cook for 4-5 minutes until soft. Add in the bacon and cook for 5 minutes. Add the potatoes, reduce the heat and stir well. Sprinkle in the cornflour then stir in the stock (broth). Pour in the cream, add the bay leaf and bring to the boil. Add the sweetcorn, reduce the heat and simmer for 15-20 minutes or until the potatoes are tender. Add the fish and prawns (shrimps) and continue cooking for around 5 minutes or until the fish is cooked through. Remove the bay leaf. Serve into bowls and enjoy.

Roast Red Pepper (Bell Pepper) Soup

Ingredients

4 red peppers (bell peppers)
1 small onion, chopped
2 cloves of garlic crushed
1 large tomato, chopped
1 carrot, chopped
1 tablespoon olive oil
600ml (1 pint) vegetable stock (broth)
600ml (1 pint) water

SERVES 4-6

Method

Heat a grill (broiler) and place the peppers underneath. Keep turning them until they are browned on all sides. Remove the peppers from the heat and allow them to cool slightly before carefully removing the skins, seeds and stalks then set aside. If you have difficulty removing the skins, place the hot peppers in a plastic bag to sweat for a few minutes which will make the skins easier to remove. Heat the oil in a saucepan and add the onion and garlic. Cook for 4 minutes. Add in the tomatoes, carrot, red peppers, water and stock (broth). Bring to the boil, reduce the heat and simmer for 30 minutes. Use a hand blender or food processor and blitz the soup until smooth. Serve and enjoy.

Cheese & Carrot Soup

Ingredients

50g (2oz) butter
2 tablespoons cornflour or plain flour
3 carrots, grated (shredded)
150g (5oz) Cheddar cheese
300ml (10fl oz) milk or non-dairy milk
400ml (14fl oz) vegetable stock (broth)
Sea salt
Freshly ground black pepper

SERVES 4

Method

Heat the butter in a saucepan then add the flour and stir continuously. Add in the stock (broth) and milk, bring to the boil then reduce the heat and simmer for a few minutes making sure the sauce is smooth and free from lumps. Add the grated carrots to the liquid and cook for 5 minutes or until the carrots have softened. Sprinkle the cheese into the soup and season with salt and pepper. Once the cheese has melted, serve and enjoy.

Beetroot Soup

Ingredients

1 onion, finely chopped

3 uncooked beetroot, peeled and finely chopped

2 apples, peeled, cored and finely chopped

2 carrots, finely chopped

900ml (1½ pints) vegetable stock (broth)

2 tablespoons olive oil

SERVES 4-6

Method

Place the oil in a saucepan, add the onion and cook for 5 minutes until it softens. Add the beetroot and carrots to the saucepan and cook for 5 minutes before adding the stock (broth) and chopped apples. Bring to the boil, reduce the heat and simmer for 20 minutes. Blend the soup until smooth or serve as it is. Pour into bowls and enjoy.

Carrot & Courgette Soup

Ingredients

3 carrots, chopped

1-2 sweet potatoes, peeled and chopped

1 onion, peeled and chopped

3 courgettes (zucchinis), chopped

600ml (1 pint) vegetable stock

1-2 tablespoons olive oil

1 teaspoon fresh thyme, chopped

1 teaspoon fresh parsley, chopped

SERVES 4

Method

Heat the olive oil in a saucepan, add the onion and cook for 5 minutes. Add all the remaining ingredients apart from the herbs. Cook for around 25 minutes, or until the vegetables are soft. Stir in the herbs. Use a hand blender or food processor and blitz until smooth. Season and serve.

Celeriac & Pear Soup

Ingredients

4 large pears, peeled and chopped
1 celeriac, peeled and chopped
1 onion, chopped
600ml (1 pint) vegetable stock (broth)
1-2 tablespoons olive oil
2 tablespoons fresh parsley, chopped
2.5cm (1 inch) chunk fresh root ginger
Sea salt
Freshly ground black pepper

SERVES
4-6

Method

Heat the olive oil in a saucepan, add the onion and cook gently for 5 minutes. Add in the celeriac, pears, ginger and stock (broth). Bring to the boil, reduce the heat and cook for 20-25 minutes and the celeriac is tender. Use a hand blender or food processor and blitz until smooth. You can add extra stock or hot water to make it thinner if you wish. Sprinkle in the parsley and season with salt and pepper.

Butternut Squash & Ginger Soup

SERVES 4

Ingredients

1 tablespoon olive oil

1 medium onion, chopped

1 butternut squash, peeled, de-seeded and chopped

1 litre (1 ½ pints) vegetable stock (broth)

1 teaspoon ground ginger or root ginger chopped

120ml (4fl oz) coconut milk

Method

Heat the oil in a saucepan, add the onion and cook until soft. Stir in the squash, ginger and stock (broth). Bring to the boil, reduce the heat and simmer until the squash is soft. Stir in the coconut milk and heat the soup thoroughly. Use a food processor or hand blender and process until smooth before serving.

Mexican Salad

Ingredients

1 head Romaine lettuce, chopped

x 400g (14oz) can pinto beans, rinsed and drained

1 medium avocado, flesh diced

1 yellow pepper (bell pepper) thinly sliced

1 medium tomato, diced

50g (2oz) cheese, grated (shredded)

1 lime, cut into wedges

Sprinkling of paprika (optional)

SERVES 2

Method

Arrange the lettuce on a plate, top with yellow pepper (bell pepper) avocado, pinto beans and tomato. Sprinkle with paprika. Top with cheese and serve with a wedge of lime. You can also add a tablespoon of salsa, see the recipe on page 109.

Tuna & Vegetable Rice

Ingredients

250g (9 oz) cooked rice
1 onion, finely chopped
2 cloves of garlic, crushed
1 green pepper (bell pepper)
1 courgette (zucchini)
3 tablespoons olive oil
1 x 160g (5 ½ oz) tin of tuna in oil

SERVES 2

Method

Heat the oil in a frying pan, add the onion, garlic, green pepper and courgette (zucchini). Cook until the vegetables have softened. Stir in the rice and mix well while warming the rice through. Add in the tuna and mix it in. Season and serve.

Quick Tortilla Pizza

Ingredients

1 wholemeal tortilla
2 tablespoons tomato based sauce,
passata or puree
3 tablespoons feta cheese
1 tablespoon olives, halved
Several basil leaves

SERVES
1

Method

Spread the tomato sauce over the tortilla and add the cheese, olives and basil. Place the tortilla under the grill (broiler) for 4 minutes and it's ready to eat. The toppings can be varied to use whatever leftovers you have ham, chicken, spinach, mushrooms, peppers, tomatoes or anything else you fancy.

Avocado & Bean Salad

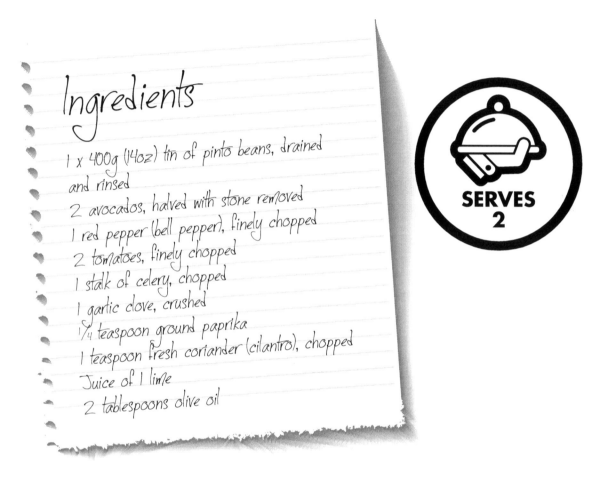

Ingredients

1 x 400g (14oz) tin of pinto beans, drained and rinsed

2 avocados, halved with stone removed

1 red pepper (bell pepper), finely chopped

2 tomatoes, finely chopped

1 stalk of celery, chopped

1 garlic clove, crushed

1/4 teaspoon ground paprika

1 teaspoon fresh coriander (cilantro), chopped

Juice of 1 lime

2 tablespoons olive oil

SERVES 2

Method

Place the lime juice in a bowl and mix with the olive oil. Stir in the pinto beans, red pepper, tomatoes, celery, coriander (cilantro), garlic and paprika. Place the avocado halves onto plates and spoon the mixture over them. Serve and enjoy.

Polenta Chips

Ingredients

175g (6oz) polenta (fine cornmeal)
75g (3oz) Parmesan cheese, grated (shredded)
750ml (1 1/4 pints) water
50g (2oz) butter
1 teaspoon salt

SERVES
2-4

Method

Bring the water to the boil and add the salt. Slowly and steadily add the polenta, stirring to pre-vent lumps from forming. Reduce the heat and simmer while stirring continuously. The polenta will thicken very quickly, in around a minute. When it does, turn off the heat. Now add the butter and Parmesan and combine. Tip the mixture into a baking dish of about 2cm (1 inch) in depth. Smooth it out. Leave it to cool for about 30 minutes or until it is set. Cut the polenta into strips, resembling chips (fries). Lay them out on a baking sheet and bake at 220C/425F for 15-20 min-utes or until they are firm and easily lift off the baking tray. Serve and enjoy.

Grilled Pears & Pecorino Cheese Salad

Ingredients

2 pears, peeled, cored and cut in half
2 large handfuls of rocket (arugula)
1 small handful of watercress
40g (1 ½ oz) pecorino cheese, shaved into slices using a peeler

Vinaigrette

50ml (2fl oz) olive oil
½ teaspoon Dijon mustard
Pinch of salt
Freshly ground black pepper

SERVES
2

Method

Combine all the ingredients for the vinaigrette in a bowl and mix well then set aside. Place the pear halves cut side down on a lined baking sheet. Top the pear halves with around half the cheese and cover them well. Place under the grill (broiler) for around 3 minutes or until they begin to bubble. In the meantime, scatter the salad leaves onto two plates and scatter the remaining pecorino throughout the salad. Sprinkle with vinaigrette. Serve the warm pears onto the salad bed. Eat immediately.

Quinoa, Avocado & Tomato Salad

SERVES 4

Ingredients

300g (11oz) quinoa
2 avocados, peeled and diced
150g (5oz) cherry tomatoes, quartered
4 tablespoons of fresh coriander (cilantro), chopped
2 tablespoons fresh parsley, chopped
1 green chilli, deseeded and finely chopped
Juice of 1 lime
Sea salt
Freshly ground black pepper

Method

Boil the quinoa for around 15 minutes, drain and leave to cool. Combine the chilli, avocado, tomatoes and lime juice in a bowl. Once the quinoa has cooled to room temperature combine it with the ingredients in the bowl. Stir in the fresh herbs and season with salt and pepper before serving.

Bacon, Spinach & Courgette 'Spaghetti'

Ingredients

2 large courgettes (zucchinis)
2 teaspoons olive oil
1 handful of spinach
4 strips of crispy bacon, cooked
and crumbled
Salt and pepper

SERVES 2

Method

Peel strips of courgette and cut them into 1cm (½ inch) wide strips or use a julienne peeler or spiralizer. Heat the olive oil in a frying pan. Add the courgette strips and cook for 2 minutes. Toss in the spinach leaves and warm them until they wilt. Sprinkle with the bacon pieces. Season with salt and pepper and serve.

DINNER

Ginger Chicken

Ingredients

4 chicken breasts
225g (8oz) mushrooms, sliced
1 bunch of spring onions (scallions)
finely chopped
3 cloves of garlic, crushed
2 ½ cm (1 inch) chunk of ginger root,
finely chopped
½ teaspoon ground cinnamon
1 tablespoon olive oil
Rind and juice of 1 orange
1 orange cut into wedges for garnish

SERVES 4

Method

Preheat the oven to 190C/375F. Heat the oil in a frying pan, add the chicken and cook for 2-3 minutes. Transfer the chicken to a casserole dish. In a bowl, mix together the garlic, cinnamon, ginger, orange juice and rind. Coat the chicken with the mixture. Add the mushrooms and spring onions (scallions) and place in the oven for 30 minutes, until the chicken is thoroughly cooked. Serve with rice and a wedge of orange to garnish.

Slow Cooked Chicken, Chorizo & Beans

Ingredients

8 chicken thighs
1 large chorizo sausage, sliced
1 x 400g (14oz) tin of chopped tomatoes
1 x 400g (14oz) tin of cannellini beans, rinsed and drained
1 onion, chopped
2 cloves of garlic, crushed
250ml (8fl oz) chicken stock (broth)
1 teaspoon tomato puree
1/2 teaspoon smoked paprika
1/2 teaspoon parsley
1 tablespoon olive oil
1 tablespoon cornflour (mixed to a smooth paste with 2-3 tablespoons of water)

SERVES 4

Method

Preheat the slow cooker for 15 minutes. Heat the olive oil in a pan, add the onions and chicken thighs and brown them on all sides for around 4 minutes. Transfer to a slow cooker. Add all the other ingredients to the slow cooker and mix well. Cook for up to 6 hours. Alternatively this casserole can be baked in the oven at 180C/360F for around 50 minutes, making sure the chicken is cooked through.

Scallops, Garlic & Parsley Butter

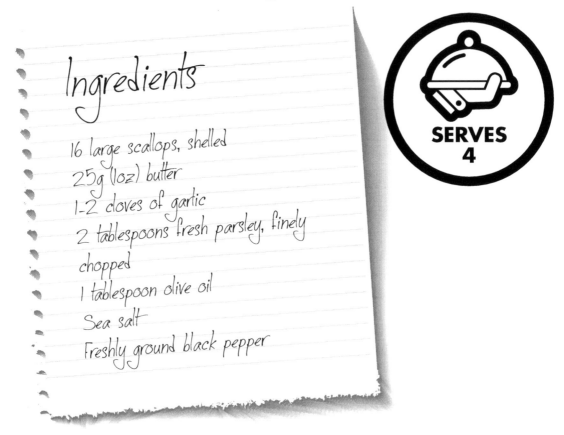

Ingredients

16 large scallops, shelled
25g (1oz) butter
1-2 cloves of garlic
2 tablespoons fresh parsley, finely chopped
1 tablespoon olive oil
Sea salt
Freshly ground black pepper

SERVES 4

Method

Place the olive oil in a frying pan over a high heat. Add the scallops and cook for around 1 minute on either side until they are slightly golden. Transfer to a dish and keep warm. Drain off any excess liquid from the pan. Gently warm the butter and the garlic for around 1 minute until the butter has melted then sprinkle in the fresh parsley. Serve the scallops and pour over the parsley butter. It's simple and delicious.

Fast Chicken Stir Fry

Ingredients

2 chicken breasts, sliced
250g (9oz) cooked rice
1 carrot, peeled and cut into strips
1 handful of green beans, washed and roughly chopped
1-2 chopped shallots, finely sliced (optional)
1 tablespoon olive oil or sesame oil
4 tablespoons tamari sauce or soy sauce
1/2 teaspoon paprika
1 red chilli, chopped (optional)
Salt and pepper
Several fresh basil leaves

SERVES 2

Method

Heat the oil in a wok or large frying pan. Add the chicken, chilli, paprika and tamari and cook for 5 minutes, stirring occasionally. Add the vegetables and cook for around 3 minutes until heated through but still crisp. Place the rice in the wok/pan and heat thoroughly. Season with salt and pepper, garnish with basil leaves and serve.

Butternut Squash Risotto

Ingredients

1 large butternut squash, peeled, de-seeded and cubed

2 cloves of garlic, crushed

225g (8oz) risotto rice (Arborio)

600ml (1 pint) warm chicken stock (broth)

40g (1 ½ oz) Parmesan cheese, grated

175g (6oz) onion, finely chopped

50g (2oz) butter

SERVES 6

Method

Melt the butter in a saucepan. Add the butternut squash and onion and gently fry until soft. Add the garlic and rice then mix well. Add in the stock (broth) a little at a time, allowing the rice to absorb most of the liquid before adding more. It will take around 20 minutes for the rice to become tender. Sprinkle with parmesan cheese and stir. Serve and enjoy.

Chicken Jambalaya

Ingredients

2 large chicken breasts, diced
12 large prawns, shelled and cooked
175g (6oz) chorizo sausage, chopped
275g (10oz) rice
1 large onion, chopped
3 cloves of garlic, chopped
2 red peppers (bell peppers), deseeded and chopped
2 stalks of celery, chopped
2 tablespoons tomato puree
2 teaspoons chilli powder, mild
1 tablespoon ground ginger
2 teaspoons Cajun seasoning
900ml (1 1/2 pints) chicken stock (broth)
4-5 tablespoons olive oil

SERVES 4

Method

Heat the oil in a frying pan, add the chicken pieces and brown them for 6-7 minutes then set aside. Add the onion and cook for until it softens. Add in the celery, garlic, tomato puree, rice and the spices and stir for 2-3 minutes. Pour in the chicken stock (broth) and simmer for around 20 minutes, or until the rice has absorbed the liquid. Add in the red peppers, prawns and cooked chicken. Cook until the prawns and chicken are heated thoroughly and the peppers have softened. Season with salt and pepper and serve.

Cod Goujons & Quick Aioli (Garlic Mayonnaise)

SERVES 2

Ingredients

2 cod fillets, cut into 2cm (1 inch) strips

2-3 cloves of garlic, crushed

1 egg, whisked

3 tablespoons plain flour

1/2 teaspoon paprika

6 tablespoons mayonnaise

1 tablespoon lemon juice and wedges

to garnish

2-3 tablespoons olive oil

Method

Place the mayonnaise in a bowl and mix in the crushed garlic and a tablespoon of lemon juice then set aside. In a bowl, combine the flour with the paprika. Dip the cod strips in the beaten egg then toss them in the flour mixture. Heat the oil in a frying pan. Add the fish strips and cook for around 4 minutes or until the goujons are golden. Serve with a wedge of lemon and the garlic dip. You could also try substituting the fish for chicken or even swap the plain flour for almond flour (ground almonds) for a gluten free option.

If you can't find a sugar-free mayonnaise, there is a recipe at the back of this book.

Roast Pork & Baked Apples

Ingredients

1.35kg (3lb) loin of pork
2 tablespoons olive oil
2 cloves of garlic, chopped
3 onions, roughly chopped
2 large sprigs of rosemary
6 apples, cored but otherwise intact
Sea salt
White pepper

SERVES 4-6

Method

Place the pork into a large ovenproof dish and make long shallow incisions in the skin with a knife. Pat dry the meat to ensure crispier crackling. Season the meat liberally with salt and pepper. Place the pork, onions, olive oil, rosemary and garlic into the ovenproof dish. Transfer to the oven and roast at 240C/475F for 25 minutes, then turn down the oven to 190C/375F and roast for 30 minutes. Put the apples next to the pork in the ovenproof dish and continue roasting for another 20 minutes. To check if the pork is cooked, insert a skewer and the juices should run clear. Allow the pork to rest for a 10 minutes before serving.

Orange Pork & Leeks

SERVES 4

Ingredients

4 pork chops
2 large leeks, thinly sliced
1 red pepper (bell pepper) sliced
150ml (5fl oz) chicken stock (broth)
3 tablespoons fresh orange juice
3 garlic cloves, crushed
1 tablespoon mustard
½ teaspoon paprika
¼ teaspoon salt
¼ teaspoon freshly ground black pepper
2 teaspoons olive oil

Method

Sprinkle the pork chops with salt, and black pepper. Heat the oil in a frying pan. Add the pork chops and fry for 3 minutes on each side or until cooked through. Remove the pork chops and keep them warm. Add to the pan the leeks, pepper (bell pepper), and garlic. Fry for 3 minutes until the leek has softened. Add in the stock (broth) orange juice, mustard, and paprika. Stir and cook for 2-3 minutes or until the liquid thickens slightly. Return the pork chops to the pan and coat them in the juices. Serve and enjoy.

Chicken Satay

Ingredients

2 skinless chicken breasts, cut into
bite-size chunks
1 teaspoon tamari sauce
4 tablespoons smooth peanut butter
2 teaspoons curry powder
200ml (7fl oz) coconut milk
1 lemon, halved
Dash of tabasco sauce

**SERVES
2**

Method

Preheat the oven to 200C/400F. In a bowl, combine the peanut butter and coconut milk. Stir in the curry powder, tabasco and tamari sauce. Thoroughly coat the chicken chunks in the peanut mixture. Thread the chicken onto skewers, and set aside the remaining satay sauce. Place the chicken skewers under a hot grill (broiler) and cook for 4-5 minutes on each side, making sure they are thoroughly cooked. Pour the remaining satay sauce into a small saucepan and add the juice from half of the lemon and bring to the boil. Cut the remaining half of the lemon into 2 wedges. Serve the chicken skewers and pour the remaining satay sauce on top. Place the lemon garnish on the side.

Menemen
(Turkish Eggs & Peppers)

Ingredients

1 x 400g (14oz) tin of chopped tomatoes
1 onion, chopped
4 peppers (bell peppers) mixture of green, red and yellow
1-2 chilies, deseeded and chopped
4 eggs
2 tablespoons fresh coriander (cilantro) chopped
1 tablespoon parsley, chopped (or fresh mint)
4-5 tablespoons olive oil
Sprinkling of cayenne pepper

SERVES 4

Method

Heat the olive oil in a frying pan and add the peppers (bell peppers) onion and chillies until the onion softens. Add the tomatoes and cook until the mixture becomes soft and pulpy, then stir in the herbs. Carefully crack each egg on top of the mixture, keeping them apart if possible to create an individual egg on each portion. Reduce the heat to prevent the bottom sticking. Co until the egg white is set and the yolks remain soft. Add extra oil or a little water if required. Sprinkle with a little cayenne pepper before serving with flatbread and Greek yogurt.

Salmon With Dill & Mustard

Ingredients

4 salmon steaks
1 tablespoon lemon juice
2 cloves of garlic, crushed
1 tablespoon Dijon mustard
3 tablespoons lemon juice
60ml (2fl oz) chicken stock (broth)
1 teaspoon fresh dill, chopped
Salt and white pepper to taste

SERVES 4

Method

Coat the salmon steaks with a tablespoon of lemon juice, salt and pepper and place under a hot grill. Cook for around 7 minutes on each side. Meanwhile, place the garlic in saucepan and cook to soften it for around a minute. Add the mustard, 2 tablespoons of lemon juice, stock (broth) salt and pepper. Bring to the boil, reduce the heat and simmer for a few minutes to reduce slightly. Sprinkle in the dill and stir. Serve the salmon along with the sauce.

Chilli Squash Boats

Ingredients

450g (1lb) minced (ground) beef or soya mince
2 butternut squashes, vertically cut in half, seeds removed
1 large onion, finely chopped
1 red pepper, finely chopped
1/2 small courgette (zucchini), finely chopped
2 garlic cloves, crushed
1 teaspoon cayenne pepper
1 teaspoon cinnamon
1 teaspoon cumin
1/2 teaspoon chilli powder, or more if you like it hotter
2 teaspoons tomato puree (paste)
1 x 400g (14oz) tin of chopped tomatoes
1 x 200g (7oz) tin of kidney beans
1 tablespoon olive oil

SERVES 4

Method

Heat the olive oil in a saucepan, add the mince and brown it for several minutes. Add in the onion, pepper, garlic and cook for 4 minutes. Add in the cayenne pepper, cumin, chilli powder, tomato puree (paste) and cinnamon and stir. Pour in the chopped tomatoes, courgette (zucchini) and kidney beans. Bring to the boil, reduce the heat and simmer for 15-20 minutes. Spoon the chilli into the hole in the squash. Cover with foil and transfer to the oven. Bake at 200C/400F for 45 minutes, until the squash is soft. Remove the foil for the last 5 minutes.

Lamb & Hummus Wraps

Ingredients

1.35kg (3lb) lamb shoulder
3 tablespoons olive oil
1/2 teaspoon ground cumin
1/2 teaspoon ground coriander
1/2 teaspoon ground cinnamon
1/2 teaspoon paprika

Hummus

1 x 400g (14oz) tin of chickpeas (garbanzo beans)
3 cloves of garlic, crushed
2 tablespoons tahini
Juice of 1 small lemon
4 tablespoons olive oil

SERVES 4

Method

Mix the spices with a tablespoon of olive oil. Coat the lamb with the mixture and marinate it for an hour, or longer if you can. Heat the remaining oil in a pan, add the lamb and brown it for 8-10 minutes on all sides to seal it. Place the lamb in an ovenproof dish and cover it with foil. Transfer to the oven and roast at 170C/325F for 4 hours. The lamb should be tender and falling off the bone. Place the chickpeas (garbanzo beans), tahini, garlic, lemon juice and olive oil into a blender and process until smooth. Serve the hummus in a bowl and sprinkling of paprika. Shred the lamb and serve onto a dish. This is an excellent meal for sharing. Place the lamb and a spoonful of hummus inside a lettuce leaf as a wrap or use a traditional tortilla wrap.

Cashew Crust Chicken

SERVES 4

Ingredients

4 chicken breasts
75g (3oz) cashew nuts
1 egg
2 tablespoons butter
1/4 teaspoon salt
1/2 teaspoon white pepper
1/2 teaspoon paprika

Method

Place the cashew nuts into a blender and process until they are powdery. Transfer them to a bowl, add the paprika, salt and pepper and mix well. In a separate bowl, beat the egg. Dip each of the chicken breasts into the egg, then dip it into the cashew nut mixture and coat thoroughly. Heat the butter in a frying pan and add the chicken. Cook for about 5-6 minutes on each side until the chicken is golden and cooked thoroughly.

Ratatouille Pasta Bake

Ingredients

300g (11oz) whole wheat pasta shells
2 tablespoons olive oil
2 onions, finely chopped
2 cloves of garlic, crushed
1 teaspoon oregano
1 teaspoon basil
4 medium tomatoes
2 large courgettes, (zucchinis) chopped
200g (7oz) broad beans
120ml (4fl oz) vegetable stock (broth)
25g (1oz) Parmesan cheese

**SERVES
4**

Method

Cook the pasta according to the instructions then drain it. Heat the olive oil in saucepan, add the onion and garlic and cook for 5 minutes until the onion is soft. Add in the courgettes (zucchinis) tomatoes, herbs and broad beans and stir for 5 minutes. Add in the stock and cook for another 5 minutes. Add the pasta shells to the vegetables and transfer to a casserole dish. Sprinkle with Parmesan and bake in the oven at 180C/350F for 20-25 minutes.

Chinese Chicken Wings

Ingredients

24 chicken wings
4 spring onions (scallions) finely chopped (optional)
1/2 teaspoon salt
1 tablespoon Chinese five-spice powder
1 tablespoon tamari sauce
1 teaspoon freshly ground black pepper

SERVES 4

Method

Place the five-spice, tamari sauce, salt and pepper into a bowl and mix well. Add the chicken wings to the marinade and coat them well with the mixture. If you have time, let them marinate for an hour or overnight if possible. When you're ready to cook them, preheat the oven to 180C/350F. Place the chicken wings on a baking tray, cover with foil and roast for 45 minutes or until they are thoroughly cooked. Remove the foil and roast for another 10-15 minutes. Serve into a bowl and sprinkle with spring onions (scallions). Can be served hot or cold.

Lamb & Black Bean Chilli

Ingredients

4 tablespoon olive oil

750g (1lb 11oz) lamb shoulder, diced

1 onion, chopped

2 chillies, deseeded and chopped

4 cloves of garlic, crushed

1/2 tablespoon ground cumin

2 x 400g (14oz) tins of chopped tomatoes

1 pint of beef or vegetable stock (broth)

2 tablespoons tomato puree

1 tablespoon dried oregano

2 x 400g tins of black beans

4 spring onions (scallions)

3 tablespoons fresh coriander (cilantro) chopped

Juice of 1 lime

SERVES 4-6

Method

Heat the oil in a saucepan, add the lamb and brown it all over then set aside. Place the onion in the pan and cook until softened. Add the chillies and garlic and cook for 2 minutes. Sprinkle in the cumin and stir. Add the tomatoes, stock (broth) tomato puree and oregano to the pan and return the lamb also. Bring to the boil, reduce the heat and simmer gently for 1 hour. Add in the black beans and continue cooking for another ½ to 1 hour. Lastly stir in the lime juice, coriander (cilantro) and spring onions (scallions). Serve with rice, or a lettuce leaf wrap with guacamole and cheese.

Herby Chicken

SERVES 4

Ingredients

4 chicken breasts
1 clove of garlic, crushed
1 tablespoon lemon juice
2 teaspoon fresh sage, chopped
2 teaspoon fresh thyme, chopped
1 teaspoon rosemary, chopped
75ml (3fl oz) chicken stock (broth)

Method

Season the chicken breasts with salt and pepper and place them under a hot grill (broiler) and cook on either side for 5-7 minutes depending on how thick the chicken is. In the meantime, place the chopped herbs, lemon juice, chicken stock (broth) and garlic into a saucepan. Bring to the boil, reduce the heat and simmer for 2 minutes. Season with salt and pepper. Slice the chicken and serve drizzled with the herby sauce.

Salmon, Herb Butter & Quinoa

Ingredients

300g (11oz) quinoa

75g (3oz) butter

2 tablespoons fresh dill, chopped

1 tablespoon fresh chives, chopped

1 lemon, rind and juice

4 salmon steaks

1 tablespoon olive oil

Sea salt

Freshly ground black pepper

SERVES 4

Method

Boil the quinoa for around 15 minutes until soft and then drain it. Combine the butter, chives, dill, lemon juice and rind. Heat the olive oil in a pan. Add the salmon steaks and cook for 3-4 minutes on each side or until cooked thoroughly. Squeeze the lemon juice into the quinoa and season with salt and pepper. Serve the salmon onto plates and top with the herb butter and a helping of quinoa on the side.

Roast Chicken, Chickpeas (Garbanzo Beans) & Butternut Squa

Ingredients

2 red onions, cut into wedges

600g (1lb 5oz) sweet potato peeled and chopped

4 tomatoes, halved

2 garlic cloves, thinly sliced

2 tablespoons olive oil

8 chicken thighs

200g (7oz) chickpeas

4 tablespoons fresh parsley, chopped

Sea salt

Freshly ground black pepper

SERVES 4

Method

In a bowl, combine the sweet potato, onion, tomato, garlic and a tablespoon of olive oil. Place the mixture in an ovenproof dish, transfer to the oven and bake at 200C/425F for 15 minutes. In the meantime, season the chicken with salt and pepper. Heat the remaining oil in a frying pan, add the chicken and seal it for 2-3 minutes each side. Place the chicken in the ovenproof dish with the vegetables and roast for 15 minutes. Stir in the chickpeas and parsley and return them to the oven. Serve when the chicken is thoroughly cooked.

Chicken & Banana Korma

Ingredients

4 chicken breasts, cubed
50g (2oz) ground almonds
1 onion, chopped
1 red chilli, de-seeded and chopped
2 cloves of garlic, crushed
1 large banana, peeled and chopped
1 tablespoon garam masala
140g (4 ½ oz) plain yogurt
5 cm (2 inch) chunk of root ginger, chopped
450ml (15fl oz) chicken stock (broth)
2 tablespoons fresh coriander (cilantro)
1 tablespoon coconut oil or olive oil
2 teaspoons cornflour

SERVES 4

Method

Place the chilli, ginger, onion and garlic into a food processor and blitz until smooth. Heat the oil in a frying pan and add the onion. Cook for 5 minutes. Stir in the garam masala. Add in the stock, ground almonds and chicken. Cover and simmer for 20-25 minutes. Stir the cornflour into the yogurt. Add the yogurt to the curry, stir and simmer until the curry thickens. Add in the chopped banana and coriander (cilantro). Cook for 5 minutes until the banana is warmed through. Serve with a sprinkling of chopped coriander (cilantro).

Prawn Balti

Ingredients

32 large prawns (shrimps), shelled and raw
2 medium onions, chopped
2 fresh chillies
3 cloves of garlic
2 tablespoons tomato puree
3 large tomatoes
2 tablespoons lemon juice
1/2 teaspoon ground coriander
1/2 teaspoon turmeric
4 tablespoons fresh coriander (cilantro) chopped
3-4 tablespoons olive oil or coconut oil

SERVES 4

Method

Place the onions, garlic, tomatoes, tomato puree (paste) chillies, lemon juice, turmeric, ground coriander (cilantro), chilli powder and two tablespoons of the fresh coriander (cilantro) into a blender and blitz until you have a smooth curry paste. Heat the olive oil in a frying pan, add the paste and cook for 3-4 minutes, stirring continuously. Add the prawns (shrimps) to the paste and cook them until they have turned pink and are thoroughly cooked. Stir in the remaining 2 tablespoons of fresh coriander (cilantro). Serve with rice.

Chicken & Vegetable Casserole

Ingredients

SERVES 4

4 chicken breasts, chopped
1 large onion, finely chopped
4 spring onions (scallions), finely chopped
4 medium carrots, peeled and chopped
100g (3 ½ oz) small button mushrooms
900g (2lb) sweet potatoes, cooked and mashed
75g (3oz) cheese, grated (shredded)
300ml (10fl oz) chicken stock (broth)
1 tablespoon fresh thyme, chopped
1 tablespoon cornflour
1 tablespoon olive oil

Method

Heat the olive oil in a frying pan and add the onion, chicken and mushrooms. Fry for 5-6 minutes then add in the carrots and stock (broth). Cook for a further 5 minutes. Sprinkle in the cornflour and stir for 2 minutes. Stir in the thyme, transfer the mixture to a casserole dish and season with salt and pepper. In a bowl combine the already cooked mashed sweet potatoes and spring onions (scallions) and season with salt and pepper. Cover the chicken and vegetable mixture with the mashed sweet potato. Sprinkle with cheese. Place the casserole in the oven at 200C/400F for around 30 minutes until the cheese has melted and is golden.

Kedgeree

SERVES 4

Ingredients

450g (1lb) smoked haddock, filleted and skin removed

175g (6oz) rice

4 hardboiled eggs, quartered

1 onion, finely chopped

1 teaspoon mild curry powder

50g (2oz) butter

1 tablespoon parsley, chopped

2 tablespoons olive oil

Method

Place the haddock in a saucepan and cover it with around a pint of water. Bring it to the boil, reduce the heat and simmer for around 8 minutes until the fish is cooked through and flaky. Drain off the fish stock (broth) and set aside. Keep the haddock warm. Place the olive oil in a saucepan, add the onion and fry it until it softens. Add in the curry powder and rice. Pour in 600ml (1 pint) of the stock you've made from poaching the fish and stir. Cook for around 10 minutes, or until the rice is soft. Break the fish into pieces and flake it through the rice. Stir in the butter and warm it until it melts. Season with salt and pepper. Add in the boiled eggs and parsley and stir to combine. Serve and enjoy.

Celeriac Cottage Pie

Ingredients

450g (1lb) minced beef (ground beef)
1 large onion, chopped
2 carrots, peeled and finely chopped
1 head of celeriac, peeled and chopped
1 leek, trimmed and finely chopped
1 x 400g (14oz) tin of chopped tomatoes
1 tablespoon Worcestershire sauce
1 tablespoon tomato puree
1 bay leaf
1 tablespoon olive oil
1 teaspoon fresh thyme, chopped
300ml (1/2 pint) beef stock (broth)

SERVES 4-6

Method

Heat the oil in a saucepan, add the beef and brown it for a few minutes. Add in the carrots and onion and cook for 8-10 minutes. Add in the tinned tomatoes, tomato puree, Worcestershire sauce, bay leaf, thyme and stock (broth). Bring to the boil, reduce the heat and simmer for 25-30 minutes. In the meantime boil the celeriac until it is soft and tender. Drain and mash it until smooth. Fry the leeks in a pan until they become soft. Combine the leeks with the mashed celeriac. Transfer the meat to a casserole dish and top it off with the mashed celeriac. Place in the oven at 200C/400F for around 30 minutes until the top is slightly golden.

Stuffed Aubergines (Eggplants)

SERVES 4

Ingredients

4 small aubergines (eggplants)
6 spring onions, chopped
4 tomatoes
2 cloves of garlic, crushed
2 tablespoons fresh basil, chopped
75g (3oz) Cheddar cheese, grated (shredded)
125g (4oz) cooked rice
2 tablespoons olive oil
1 teaspoon tomato puree (paste)
Sea salt
Freshly ground black pepper

Method

Halve the aubergines (eggplants) and scoop out the flesh, making sure that you keep the outer skin around 1cm (approx ½ inch) thick. Sprinkle the skins with salt and leave upside down on kitchen paper for 5 minutes to get rid of excess water. Chop the aubergine flesh and let it sit in a colander to drain off any excess water. Heat the olive oil in a frying pan and add the aubergine flesh, tomatoes, garlic, spring onions, tomato puree, rice and basil. Cook for 5 minutes. Season with salt and pepper. Spoon the rice and vegetable mixture into the aubergine (eggplant) skins. Sprinkle with cheese. Transfer to the oven and bake at 180C/350F for around 30 minutes.

Pesto Salmon & Courgette 'Spaghetti'

Ingredients

- 2 salmon fillets
- 6 tablespoons red pepper pesto (see the recipe on page 107)
- 2 large courgettes (zucchinis)
- 1-2 tablespoons olive oil

SERVES 2

Method

Coat the salmon fillets in the red pepper pesto. Heat 2 tablespoons of the olive oil in a frying pan. Cook the salmon for 4-5 minutes on each side until the fish changes colour. In the meantime, use a vegetable peeler and peel thin strips off the courgette (zucchini). Remove the salmon from the pan and keep warm. Add a little extra oil to the frying pan if necessary. Place the courgette strips in the pan and cook for 2-3 minutes until soft. Season with salt and pepper. Serve the courgette spaghetti onto plates and place the salmon on top.

Thai Chicken Noodles

Ingredients

300g (11oz) egg noodles
400g (14oz) cooked chicken (leftovers are perfect)
2 tablespoons thai red curry paste
1 x 400ml (14fl oz) tin of coconut milk
1 onion, thinly sliced
4 cloves of garlic, crushed
1 teaspoon fish sauce
250ml (8fl oz) chicken stock (broth)
3 tablespoons fresh coriander (cilantro) chopped
1 teaspoon turmeric
Juice of ½ lime
2-3 tablespoons olive oil or groundnut oil

SERVES 4

Method

Heat the oil in saucepan, add the onion and cook until it softens. Add the garlic, turmeric and red curry paste. Cook for 1-2 minutes before adding the stock (broth), coconut milk and fish sauce. Bring to the boil then reduce the heat and simmer for 10 minutes. Add the cooked chicken and cook for 5 minutes making sure the chicken is heated thoroughly. Stir in the lime juice and coriander, holding back a few leaves for garnishing. Boil the egg noodles according to the instructions then serve them into bowls. Serve the curry on top of the noodles with a sprinkling of coriander. Enjoy.

Spare Ribs

Ingredients

1kg (2lb 4oz) pork ribs, individually cut
1 large onion, chopped
2 cloves of garlic
2.5cm (1 inch) chunk of ginger root
1-2 chillies, de-seeded
5 tablespoons tamari sauce
2 teaspoons smoked paprika
1/2 teaspoon cinnamon
3 tablespoons lemon juice
2 tablespoons ground nut oil
Sea salt
Freshly ground black pepper

SERVES 4

Method

Place the pork ribs in a roasting tin or baking tray and cook them in the oven at 180C/350F for around 25 minutes. Place the lemon juice, oil, paprika, cinnamon, garlic, onion, ginger, tamari and chilli into a blender and blitz until smooth. Season with salt and pepper. Transfer the mixture to a saucepan and cook for 5-6 minutes. Cover the cooked ribs with the sauce, making sure they're evenly coated. Return the ribs to the oven and cook for 10 minutes. Alternatively place them on a pre-heated barbecue, turning to ensure even cooking until cooked thoroughly. Place on a large serving plate and eat them while hot.

Steak & Watercress

SERVES 2

Ingredients

2 sirloin steaks
Handful of fresh watercress
40g (1 ½ oz) butter
½ teaspoon cayenne pepper
(more if you prefer it hotter)
Sea salt
Freshly ground black pepper

Method

Chop the watercress very finely and place 2 tablespoons of it into a bowl. Add the butter and combine with the chopped watercress, making sure it's mixed really well. Sprinkle the steaks with cayenne pepper and season with salt and pepper. Heat a little oil in a pan, add the steaks and cook to your liking. As a guide; 1 ½ minutes each side for rare, 2 minutes each side for medium rare and 2 ½ minutes each side for medium. Well done steaks take between 4 and 5 minutes. Allow the steak to rest for a few minutes while keeping them warm. Serve with a dollop of watercress butter and a sprinkling of fresh watercress to garnish.

Crab Cakes & Tomato Salsa

SERVES 2

Ingredients

250g (9 oz) crabmeat

2 small red chillies, de-seeded

1 clove of garlic, crushed

2.5cm (1 inch) chunk of ginger root, chopped

2 tablespoons fresh coriander (cilantro)

1 egg white

2 tablespoons olive oil

Method

Place the all the ingredients, apart from the oil, into a food processor and blend until everything is combined. Form the crab cake mixture into patties and chill for half an hour or so. Heat the oil in a frying pan and add the crab cakes. Cook for 3-4 minutes on either side until golden brown. Serve with a generous helping of tomato salsa. For the salsa, see the recipe on page 109.

SNACKS, DESSERTS & SWEET TREATS

Toasted Paprika Almonds

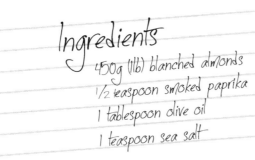

Ingredients
450g (1lb) blanched almonds
1/2 teaspoon smoked paprika
1 tablespoon olive oil
1 teaspoon sea salt

Method

Lightly coat the almonds in olive oil and lay them on a baking sheet. Roast in the oven at 200C/400F for 8 minutes. Combine the paprika and salt in a bowl. Remove the almonds from the oven, toss them in the paprika. Serve them as a healthy, tasty snack

Lime & Chilli Chickpeas (Garbanzo Beans)

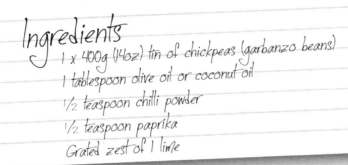

Ingredients
1 x 400g (14oz) tin of chickpeas (garbanzo beans)
1 tablespoon olive oil or coconut oil
1/2 teaspoon chilli powder
1/2 teaspoon paprika
Grated zest of 1 lime

Method

Place the chickpeas (garbanzo beans) in a bowl and coat with oil. Spread them on a baking sheet. Place in the oven at 200C/400F for 40 minutes until the chickpeas are crisp. Serve them into a bowl, sprinkle with paprika, chilli powder and lime zest. Mix well and enjoy.

Courgette (Zucchini) Fritters

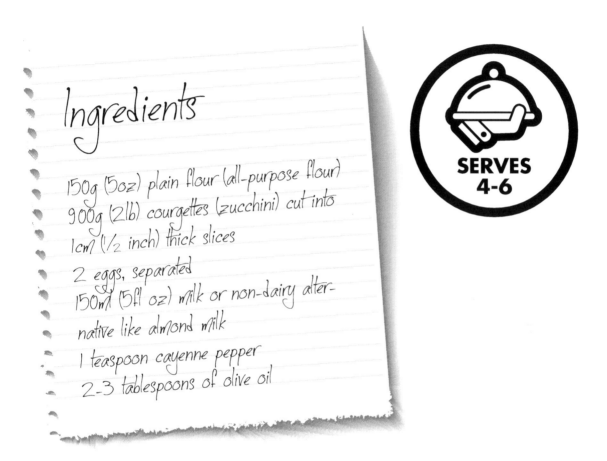

Ingredients

150g (5oz) plain flour (all-purpose flour)
900g (2lb) courgettes (zucchini) cut into
1cm (1/2 inch) thick slices
2 eggs, separated
150ml (5fl oz) milk or non-dairy alternative like almond milk
1 teaspoon cayenne pepper
2-3 tablespoons of olive oil

SERVES 4-6

Method

Sprinkle the courgettes (zucchinis) with a little salt and blot with kitchen paper to remove the excess juice from the vegetable then set aside. Place the flour in a bowl and stir in the milk, a tablespoon of olive oil and the 2 egg yolks. Stir well until you have a smooth batter. Beat the egg whites until they form stiff peaks. Now gently fold the egg whites into the batter. Sprinkle in the cayenne pepper. Thoroughly coat the courgettes in the batter. Heat the remaining oil in frying pan and add the courgette fritters. Cook for 1-2 minutes on either side, or until golden. Serve hot and enjoy.

Sesame Biscuits

Ingredients

2 tablespoons sesame seeds

1 egg

25g (1oz) butter

150g (5oz) plain flour

1-2 tablespoons fresh thyme, finely chopped

3 tablespoons water

1 teaspoon grated lemon rind

1/2 teaspoon sea salt

Sprinkling of white pepper

Extra sesame seeds for garnish

MAKES APPROX 25

Method

In a bowl, place the flour, lemon rind, thyme, sesame seeds, salt and pepper. Cut the butter into flakes and add to the flour mixture. Rub in the butter until it is mixed in completely. Pour in the water a little at a time, until the mixture binds together and forms dough. Place the dough on a floured flat surface and roll it out. Us a cutter and cut the dough into rounds. Place them onto a baking sheet, brush with the egg white and sprinkle with sesame seeds. Bake at 190C/375F for 20-25 minutes until golden.

Beetroot Chips

Ingredients

2 raw beetroot
1 tablespoon olive oil
Sea salt
White pepper

SERVES
2

Method

Peel the beetroot and cut it into thin slices of no more than 2-3mm thick. Coat the beetroot with olive oil and season with salt and pepper. Lay the beetroot slices out in a single layer onto a lightly greased baking tray. Transfer to the oven and bake at 200C/400F for 10 minutes, or until the beetroot chips are crisp. Let them sit on kitchen paper to drain off excess oil. Serve with a selection of dips.

Rice Pudding With Cinnamon & Nuts

**SERVES
4**

Ingredients

50g (2oz) hazelnuts, chopped

50g (2oz) pecan nuts, chopped

125g (4oz) risotto rice

50g (2oz) butter

600ml (1 pint warm milk or

non-dairy alternative

1 banana

1-2 teaspoons stevia powder (optional)

1 teaspoon ground cinnamon

Method

Heat a frying pan, add the nuts and toast until golden, then set aside. Heat the butter in a saucepan, stir in the rice and cook for around 1 minute. Slowly add the warm milk to the rice, stirring continuously. Add the cinnamon and simmer gently for around 20 minutes. Mash the banana and stir it into the rice pudding at the end of cooking and warm it through. Taste the rice pudding and add some stevia is you want it sweeter. Serve the rice pudding into bowls and sprinkle with the toasted nuts.

Raspberry Fool

Ingredients

350g (12oz) raspberries
175ml (6fl oz) whipping cream (heavy cream) or crème fraiche
175ml (6fl oz) plain unflavoured yogurt
1-2 teaspoons stevia (optional, depending on how sweet the raspberries are)
Extra raspberries to garnish

SERVES 4

Method

Place the raspberries into a blender and puree them. If you require extra sweetness mix in the stevia powder. Push the raspberry puree through a sieve to remove all of the seeds. Whip the cream until thick then combine it with the yogurt. Mix the raspberry puree with the cream and yogurt. Spoon the dessert into decorative glasses and top with a few raspberries. Chill before serving.

Apple Crumble

SERVES 4-6

Ingredients

6 apples, peeled, cored and chopped
1 teaspoon ground cinnamon
1/2 teaspoon nutmeg
100g (3 1/2 oz) butter
225g (8oz) almond flour
5 tablespoons coconut oil
Vanilla extract or vanilla pod

Method

Place the chopped apples in an ovenproof dish and sprinkle them with cinnamon and nutmeg. Place the flour, coconut oil and butter in a bowl with the vanilla and nutmeg. Combine by rubbing the mixture between your fingers to form the crumbly topping. Cover the apples with the topping. Bake in the oven at 180C/350F for 45 minutes, or until the topping is crispy and the apple sauce is bubbling up. Serve with crème fraiche or plain yogurt.

Banana Biscuits

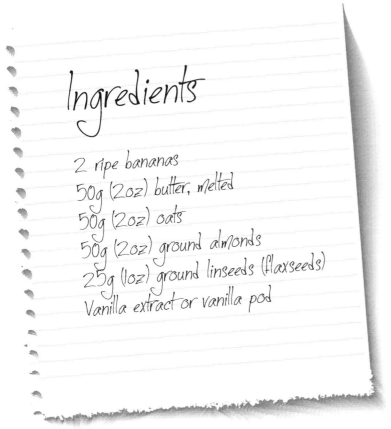

Ingredients

2 ripe bananas
50g (2oz) butter, melted
50g (2oz) oats
50g (2oz) ground almonds
25g (1oz) ground linseeds (flaxseeds)
Vanilla extract or vanilla pod

MAKES APPROX
20

Method

Mash up the bananas in a large bowl and mix with the melted butter and vanilla. Add all of the remaining ingredients and combine. Leave to stand for 10 minutes and the mixture will firm up. Use a teaspoon to scoop out the dough. Roll it into balls and then pat down on a greased or lined baking tray. Bake at 180C/350F for 15-20 minutes or until golden brown.

Chocolate Bites

Ingredients

75g (3oz) butter

75g (3oz) coconut oil

2 tablespoons cocoa powder

1-2 teaspoons stevia

3 tablespoons desiccated (shredded) coconut

MAKES APPROX 20

Method

Heat the butter, stevia and coconut oil, in a saucepan and stir until the stevia has dissolved. Place the cocoa powder in a bowl and stir in a tablespoon of the butter/oil to make a smooth paste then pour in the rest of the butter/oil and mix thoroughly. Use either a chocolate mould or an ice cube tray. Sprinkle a little of the coconut into each mould to line it ready for the chocolate to go on top. Add the chocolate mixture to the fill level of the moulds. Chill in the fridge until completely set.

Alternatively you could try adding a few drops of orange oil, vanilla or chopped nuts to the chocolate mixture, finishing off with ground almonds. Or you could try pouring the chocolate into the mould and popping a raspberry into the middle, making sure it's well covered by the chocolate then leave it to set.

Chocolate Cupcakes

Ingredients

125g (4oz) almond flour
½ butternut squash, cooked and mashed
60ml (2fl oz) coconut oil (melted)
2 tablespoons ground linseeds (flaxseeds)
1 tablespoon peanut butter or almond butter
1-2 tablespoons 100% cocoa powder
½ teaspoon bicarbonate of soda/baking soda

**MAKES
6**

Method

In a bowl stir together the almond flour, flaxseeds, bicarbonate of soda and cocoa powder. In a separate bowl, mix the squash, coconut oil and nut butter. Stir the squash mixture into the dry ingredients and mix well. Spoon the mixture into a 6 hole muffin tin and transfer to the oven. Bake at 180C/350F for 30 minutes. Test with a skewer which will come out clean when they're cooked.

Mixed Fruit Kebabs & Strawberry Coulis

SERVES 2

Ingredients

¼ pineapple, peeled and cubed
1 banana, peeled and cut into chunks
1 pear, peeled and cut into chunks
½ teaspoon ground cinnamon
225g (8oz) fresh strawberries
Juice of 1 small orange

Method

Place the strawberries and orange juice into a blender and blitz until smooth then set aside. Preheat the grill (broiler). Thread the fruit chunks alternately onto skewers. Sprinkle with cinnamon, and place them under the grill for 8 minutes, turning once half way through. Serve hot and drizzle with strawberry coulis. Enjoy.

Strawberry Mousse

SERVES
2

Ingredients

200g (7oz) strawberries, hulled and halved
1 vanilla pod
125g (4oz) tofu, silken or firm

Method

Place the strawberries in a small pan and simmer for 10-15 minutes. The strawberries are ready when they are completely soft. Set aside to cool. Place the strawberries, tofu and vanilla into a blender and process until smooth. Spoon it into decorative glasses or bowls and chill before serving.

Summer Berry & Passion Fruit Salad

SERVES
6

Ingredients

Juice of 1/2 lemon
150g (5oz) raspberries
150g (5oz) blueberries

150g (5oz) redcurrants
and/or blackcurrants
450g (1lb strawberries)
2 passion fruits

Method

Place all the berries in a bowl and mix them. Slice the passion fruit in half and scoop out the flesh and seeds onto the mixed fruit. Squeeze the lemon juice over the fruit and gently toss everything together. Serve and enjoy.

Superfast Chocolate Orange Cheesecake

SERVES 2

Ingredients

8 oat cakes (sugar-free)
250g (9oz) cream cheese
1 large orange, cut into segments
1 teaspoon stevia powder
2 teaspoons 100% cocoa powder

Method

Combine the cream cheese with the orange and stevia powder. Crumble the oat biscuits and sprinkle half of them into two glasses. Next add a layer of cream cheese mixture. Sprinkle half of the cocoa powder into the glasses. Repeat with another layer of oat biscuits, a layer of cream cheese and another sprinkling of cocoa powder.

Apple & Cinnamon Fritters

Ingredients

4 large apples, peeled, cored and sliced

1/2 teaspoon cinnamon

150g (5oz) plain flour

2 eggs, separated

150ml (5fl oz) regular milk or almond milk

2-3 tablespoons of olive oil

MAKES 4-6

Method

Place the flour and cinnamon in a bowl and stir in the milk, a tablespoon of olive oil and the egg yolks. Stir well until you have a smooth batter. In a separate bowl, beat the egg whites until they form stiff peaks. Now gently fold in the egg whites to the batter and combine. Dip the apple slices in the batter. Heat the oil in frying pan and add the apple fritters. Cook for 1-2 minutes on either side, or until golden. Serve hot with crème fraiche plain yogurt or sugar-free ice cream and enjoy.

Banana Ice Cream

Ingredients
600ml (1 pint) full-fat coconut milk
2 ripe avocados
2 ripe bananas

SERVES
2-3

Method

Place all the ingredients into a food processor or use a hand blender and blitz until smooth. Pour the mixture into an ice-cream maker and process according to the instructions for your model of machine. Serve straight away or freeze it. If you don't have an ice cream maker, place it in the freezer and occasionally whisk with a fork while it's freezing.

Almond Hot Chocolate

Ingredients
200ml (7fl oz) coconut milk
100ml (3 1/2 fl oz) rice or almond milk
1 tablespoon almond butter
1 1/2 teaspoons 100% cocoa powder
1/2 to 1 teaspoons stevia (optional)

SERVES
1

Method

Place the milk, nut butter and cocoa powder in a saucepan and mix well. Warm the milk to boiling point, reduce the heat and simmer for 1 minute. Whisk it really well to make it frothy. Pour into a mug and if required, sweeten with stevia, however some find the combination of coconut milk and rice milk make the drink sweet enough.

Orange & Raspberry Fruity Water

Ingredients

3 pints of water
1 orange, thinly sliced
1 handful of raspberries
1-2 cups of ice cubes

Method

A great replacement for fizzy, sugary drinks is fruit infused water. Fill a glass jug with water, add a small amount of fruit together with some ice and refrigerate it for 2-3 hours. You will only need a small amount of fruit, even less for stronger ingredients such as fennel and herbs. Experiment with some of these tasty combinations

Cucumber and Fresh Mint	Orange & Fennel
Strawberry & Lime	Apricot & Raspberry
Kiwi & Lemon	Lime & Cucumber
Cherry & Apple	Orange & Thyme
Apple, Ginger & Cinnamon	Lemon & Ginger
Mango & Mint	Pineapple, Cherry & Lemon

SAUCES
AND
DIPS

Tomato & Herb Sauce

Ingredients

3 cloves of garlic, crushed
2 onions, finely chopped
3 x 400g (14oz) tins of tomatoes
1 red pepper, chopped
1 large handful of mixed herbs; oregano,
basil and thyme
1 tablespoon olive oil
Salt
Freshly ground black pepper

Method

Heat the olive oil in a pan. Add the garlic and onions. Cook until soft and translucent. Pour in the tomatoes and add the red pepper to the onions and add the mixed herbs. Season with salt and pepper. This makes a large batch which can be frozen and used for pasta sauces and pizza toppings.

Sweet Red Pepper Pesto

Ingredients

4 large red peppers
3 cloves of garlic
75g (3oz) basil leaves
2 tablespoons olive oil
Sea salt
Freshly ground black pepper

Method

Place the peppers under a hot grill (broiler) and keep turning them until charred on all sides. Remove the skin, seeds and stalk. If you have difficulty removing the skin, place the hot peppers in a plastic bag to sweat for a few minutes which will make them easier to remove. Place all of the ingredients into a food processor or use a hand blender and blitz until smooth. Season with salt and pepper.

Aioli (Garlic Mayonnaise)

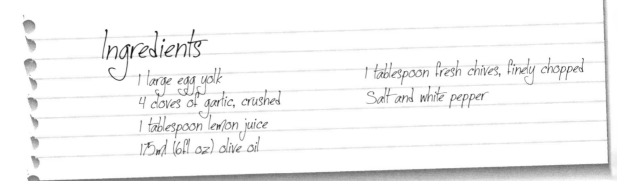

Ingredients

1 large egg yolk
4 cloves of garlic, crushed
1 tablespoon lemon juice
175ml (6fl oz) olive oil

1 tablespoon fresh chives, finely chopped
Salt and white pepper

Method

Whisk the egg yolk and add the garlic and lemon juice. Season with salt and pepper. Slowly add the olive oil, until you have a smooth thick sauce and add the chives. This is the long version in case your usual mayo has sugar.

Tapenade

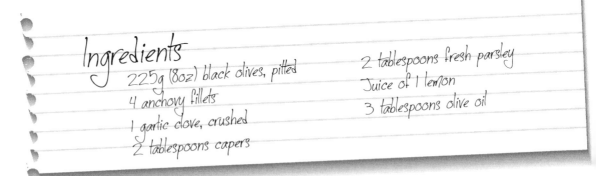

Ingredients

225g (8oz) black olives, pitted
4 anchovy fillets
1 garlic clove, crushed
2 tablespoons capers

2 tablespoons fresh parsley
Juice of 1 lemon
3 tablespoons olive oil

Method

Combine olives, garlic, capers, parsley, anchovy, lemon juice, and black pepper in a food processor or a bowl and blend to a thick paste. Add the olive oil and mix well. Serve with crackers or vegetable chips.

Pineapple Salsa

Ingredients

1 small pineapple, peeled and finely chopped
1 small red onion, finely chopped
2.5cm (1 inch) chunk of fresh ginger, peeled and finely chopped

½ teaspoon garam masala
½ teaspoon ground cumin
1 tablespoon coriander leaves or mint, finely chopped

Method

Combine all of the ingredients in a bowl and chill for 30 minutes before serving.

Tomato Salsa

Ingredients

½ red onion, finely chopped
2 ripe tomatoes, finely chopped
1 tablespoon fresh coriander (cilantro), finely chopped

2 tablespoons lemon juice
1 red chili, deseeded and finely chopped
1 clove of garlic, crushed
1 tablespoon olive oil

Method

Combine all of the ingredients in a bowl and chill before serving. Use as an accompaniment to fish, chicken or meat dishes and salads.

Printed in Great Britain
by Amazon